T0046748

ORDINARY PEOPLE CHANGE THE WORLD

# I am Marie Curie

BRAD MELTZER

illustrated by Christopher Eliopoulos

ROCKY POND BOOKS

I am MARIE CURIE.

When I was four years old in Poland, this was one of my favorite treasures: my dad's glass cabinet, filled with scientific instruments. I used to stare at it, wondering about each item.

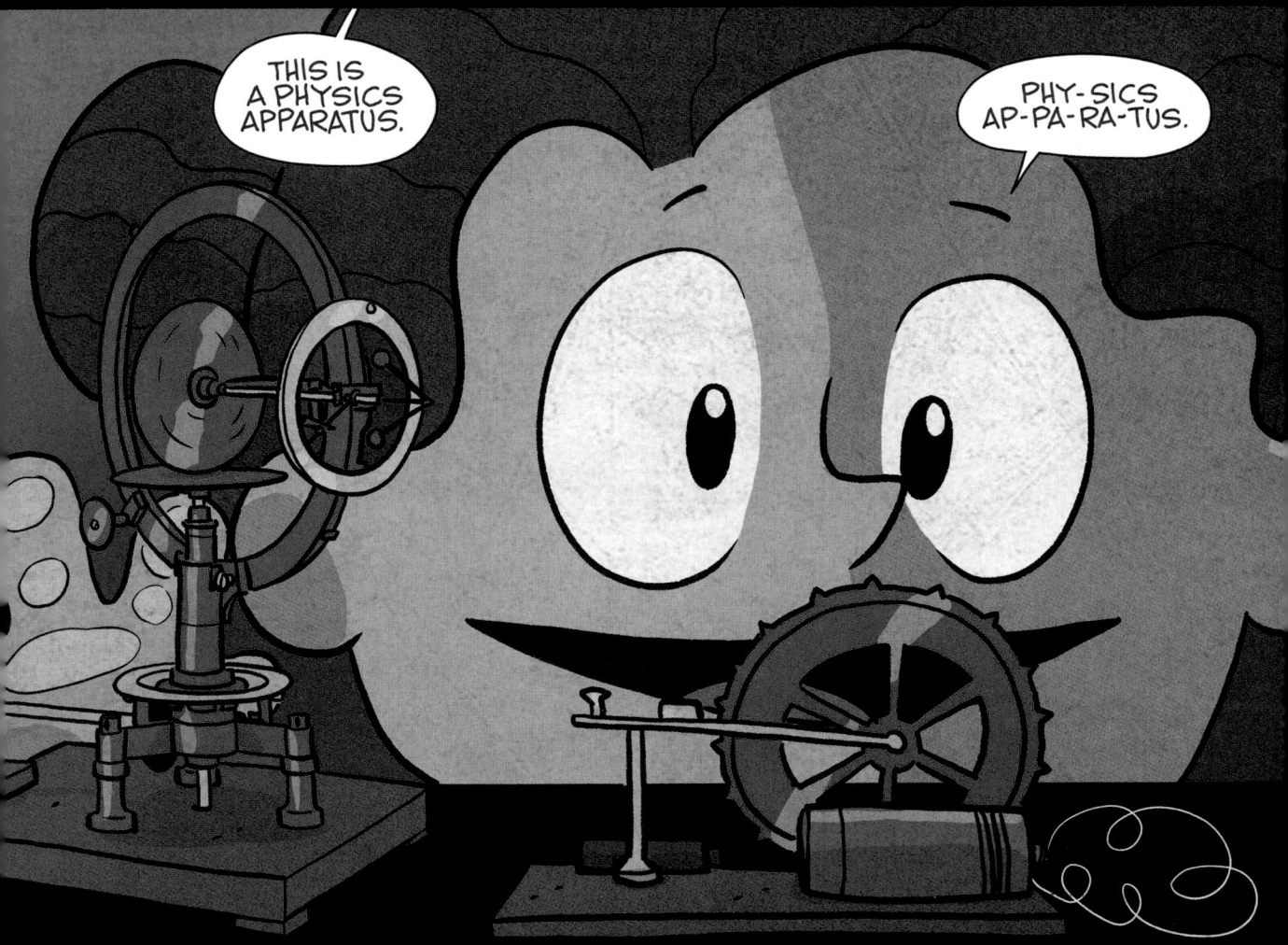


I didn't know what the words meant.
But I'd never forget them.

As a science teacher, my father needed these tools. But the Russian government soon shut down laboratory classes in our schools.

They didn't want Polish kids to learn about science. They thought education would be dangerous—that it would make us powerful.

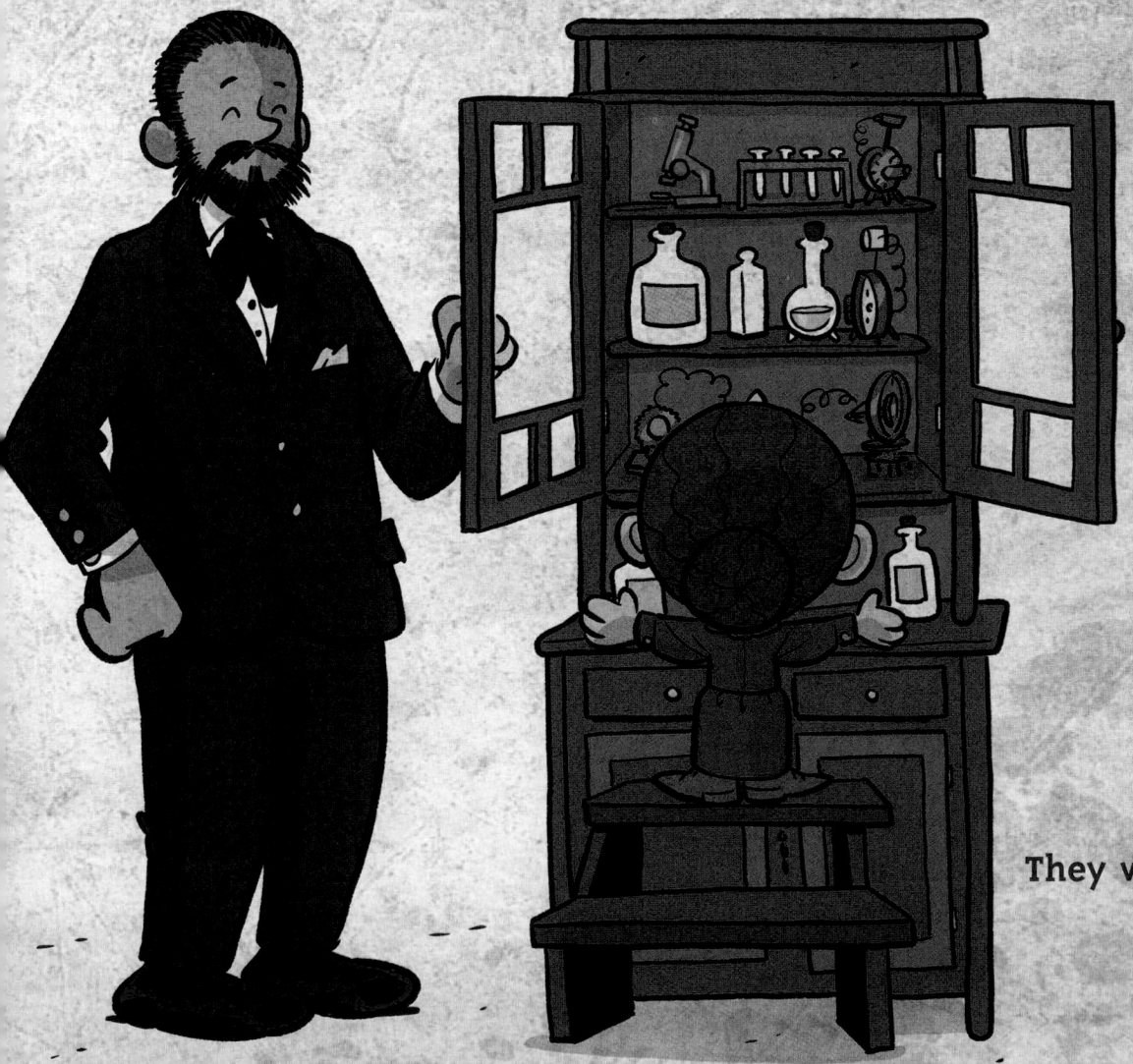

They were right.

I really liked learning.

One day, when my older sister was struggling to read, I picked up her book and read the first sentence easily.

From the looks on everyone's faces, I thought I'd made a mistake.

Back then, men didn't think girls could be good students, and they certainly didn't think we could be scientists.

So boys were always trying to challenge me.

From the very start, there was one person who always believed in me: my dad.

When my mom got sick, he took care of us kids.

Since he was a teacher, even if we were just taking a walk, he'd give us a new scientific lesson.

Back then, we didn't have phones, TVs, or computers.

So our Saturday nights were spent with Dad sharing one of the most powerful things of all: books.

He'd read us classics like *David Copperfield* and one of my favorites, *A Tale of Two Cities*.

Growing up, life was hard.

My mom and one of my sisters passed away.

My father wasn't allowed to teach the subject he loved.

We didn't have much money.

To escape the hard times, I would read...

draw...

and dance.
ONE NIGHT I DANCED SO LONG, I COMPLETELY WORE OUT MY SHOES.

At fifteen, I graduated from high school early.

I won the gold medal for being the first in my class.

By sixteen, I knew I wanted to make an impact on this world.

I even knew how.

There was only one problem.

Where I lived, the university didn't accept women.
I'M SORRY. NO GIRLS ALLOWED.
THAT'S NOT FAIR.
They wouldn't let me in.
But I had my own ideas.

Lucky for me, someone started a secret college where they taught women subjects that no one else would teach us.
It was called the "Flying University."
THE PERIODICITY OF THE ELEMENTS
THAT'S THE COOLEST NAME, RIGHT?
THE COLLEGE DIDN'T REALLY FLY.
BUT WITH MORE THAN 1,000 WOMEN ENROLLED, IT WAS MAGICAL!
AND POWERFUL!

THIS IS CALLED THE PERIODIC TABLE.
IT LISTS EVERY ELEMENT WE KNOW, LIKE HYDROGEN, OXYGEN...

Eventually, my sister Bronya and I made a plan.

We would save enough money to go to the Sorbonne in France, one of the most famous universities in the world.

But we didn't have enough money for both of us.

Every day, I was so determined to become a scientist.

I'd wake up at six a.m. and read books in three different languages on physics and anatomy.

Then I'd do the math problems my dad would send for me to solve.

By the time I was eighteen, I was doing my own experiments and drawing my own conclusions.

I also learned one of the most valuable lessons of all: You should never accept everything as it is. Life, like science, can always be made better.

I had lots of accidents and failures.

Making change is never easy.

It takes hard work.

Finally, when I was twenty-three, my dream came true.
I became a student at the Sorbonne.
I would dedicate my life to science.
YOU SURE YOU KNOW WHAT YOU'RE GETTING INTO?
ABSOLUTELY.

I felt like a new person with new power.

When I got there, I even signed the registration book differently.

Like I said, making change isn't easy.

I had to climb six flights of stairs to get to my room.

It had a tiny stove, and there wasn't much to eat.

In the winter, it was so cold that water would freeze in the basin.

I'd have to sleep under all my clothes.

I KNOW IT SOUNDS HARD, BUT IT WAS WORTH IT TO BE ABLE TO STUDY WHAT I WANTED.
THESE WERE SOME OF THE BEST YEARS OF MY LIFE.

The Sorbonne's School of Science had 2,000 students.
Only twenty-three were women.

And only two of us were studying science.

I was so nervous during my first exam, I could barely read it.
But when the professor announced our scores...

In 1893, I got my degree in physics.
A year later, I got a second degree in mathematics.

Soon after, I got married—to a scientist, of course.

Back then, people thought that men were supposed to get jobs, and women were supposed to stay home.

Again, I had my own ideas.

The only thing you're *supposed* to do is chase what you love.

This was my next lab, a crowded, damp storeroom.
I started studying a chemical element called uranium.

My husband found my research so exciting, he put aside his own work to join me.

Together, we discovered two brand-new elements: polonium and radium.

Those ideas—based on my research—changed the way the world looked at atoms and radioactivity.

In 1903, I was nominated, along with my husband and another scientist named Henri Becquerel, for the Nobel Prize in Physics, one of the most prestigious awards in science.

Eventually, I became the first woman professor at the Sorbonne.

Then my lab became the top place in the world for studying radium and measuring radioactivity.

From there, I won a second Nobel Prize—by myself—this time in chemistry.

I was the first person to ever receive Nobel Prizes in two fields.

Then I invented mobile X-ray units, to help treat soldiers during World War I.

In the United States, I even got invited to the White House, where President Harding presented me with one gram of radium in a locked box.

It was worth more than one hundred thousand dollars, a gift from the women in America, who'd collected money so I could continue my groundbreaking work.

In my life, I was told that
only boys could be educated,
only boys should study science,
and only boys would win awards.
I had other ideas.

Don't let anyone limit what you can achieve.
It's easy to follow the crowd and do what's been done before.
But to forge your own path, you have to be daring.
You have to risk failure.
That's how you learn.
Education is like a magic key.
It unlocks knowledge.

And with that knowledge...

You have power.

DID YOU KNOW HER FACE IS ON FRENCH MONEY?
THE 500-FRANC NOTE.
TODAY, THERE ARE MANY AMAZING WOMEN SCIENTISTS.
AND THERE CAN BE EVEN MORE.
JOIN US!
YOUR EXPERIMENTS AND IDEAS CAN HELP CHANGE THE WORLD.

Science taught me to ask questions,
experiment,
fail,
try again,
and then try some more.
You won't always find the answers you expect, and that's okay.
You will find new information, new questions, new possibilities.

ELIZABETH BLACKBURN
BIOLOGIST

SALLY RIDE
ASTRONAUT

MAE JEMISON
ASTRONAUT

GRACE HOPPER
COMPUTER SCIENTIST

DOROTHY HODGKIN
CHEMIST

I am Marie Curie.
I know the power of discovery.
KATHERINE JOHNSON
MATHEMATICIAN
LISE MEITNER
PHYSICIST

*"Nothing in life is to be feared. It is only to be understood."*
**—MARIE CURIE**

## Timeline

| NOVEMBER 7, 1867 | 1891 | JULY 26, 1895 | JULY 18, 1898 | JULY 26, 1898 |
|---|---|---|---|---|
| Born in Warsaw, Poland, as Maria Sklodowska | Registers at the Sorbonne under the name Marie | Marries Pierre Curie | Invents the term *radioactivity* and announces discovery of polonium | Announces discovery of radium |

Marie with Pierre

Marie as a child (middle), with siblings (left to right) Zosia, Hela, Joseph, and Bronya

Marie teaching at the Sorbonne

Marie in her laboratory

**DECEMBER 1903**
Wins Nobel Prize in physics

**NOVEMBER 5, 1906**
Becomes first woman professor at the Sorbonne

**1911**
Wins Nobel Prize in chemistry

**JULY 4, 1934**
Dies in France, from longtime exposure to radiation

**1995**
Reburied in the French Pantheon

*For Chris Weiss,*
*my favorite doctor.*
*Hope your daughters are impressed.*
*You owe me five bucks.*
*And thanks for one of the*
*greatest friendships of my life.*
–B.M.

*For Morgan and Christopher,*
*You can do anything,*
*be anything,*
*achieve anything.*
–C.E.

## SOURCES

*Obsessive Genius: The Inner World of Marie Curie* by Barbara Goldsmith (Norton, 2005)
*Pierre Curie* by Marie Curie (Dover, 2012)
*Marie Curie: Mother of Modern Physics* by Janice Borzendowski (Sterling, 2009)
*Madame Curie—A Biography* by Eve Curie
American Institute of Physics: https://history.aip.org/history/exhibits/curie/polgirl1.htm

## FURTHER READING FOR KIDS

*Who Was Marie Curie?* by Megan Stine (Penguin Workshop, 2014)
*Marie Curie* by Demi (Henry Holt, 2018)
*She Persisted Around the World* by Chelsea Clinton (Philomel, 2018)

ROCKY POND BOOKS | An imprint of Penguin Random House LLC, New York

First published in the United States of America by Dial Books for Young Readers, an imprint of Penguin Random House LLC, 2019
This edition published by Rocky Pond Books, an imprint of Penguin Random House LLC, 2023

Text copyright © 2019 by Forty-four Steps, Inc.
Illustrations copyright © 2019 by Christopher Eliopoulos

Penguin supports copyright. Copyright fuels creativity, encourages diverse voices, promotes free speech, and creates a vibrant culture. Thank you for buying an authorized edition of this book and for complying with copyright laws by not reproducing, scanning, or distributing any part of it in any form without permission. You are supporting writers and allowing Penguin to continue to publish books for every reader.

Rocky Pond Books & colophon are trademarks of Penguin Random House LLC.
The Penguin colophon is a registered trademark of Penguin Books Limited.

Visit us online at penguinrandomhouse.com.

LIBRARY OF CONGRESS CATALOGING-IN-PUBLICATION DATA
Names: Meltzer, Brad, author. | Eliopoulos, Chris, illustrator. | Title: I am Marie Curie / by Brad Meltzer; illustrated by Christopher Eliopoulos.
Other titles: Ordinary people change the world.
Description: New York: Dial Books for Young Readers, [2019] | Series: Ordinary people change the world | "Dial Books for Young Readers: an imprint of Penguin Random House LLC."
Audience: Ages 5–8. | Audience: K to grade 3. | Identifiers: LCCN 2019008249 | ISBN 9780525555858 (hardcover) | Subjects: LCSH: Curie, Marie, 1867–1934—Juvenile literature.
Radioactivity—History—Juvenile literature. | Women chemists—France—Biography—Juvenile literature. | Women physicists—France—Biography—Juvenile literature.
Chemists—France—Biography—Juvenile literature. | Physicists—France—Biography—Juvenile literature. | Women Nobel Prize winners—Biography—Juvenile literature.
Nobel Prize winners—Biography—Juvenile literature. | Classification: LCC QD22.C8 M45 2019 | DDC 540.92—dc23 LC | record available at https://lccn.loc.gov/2019008249

Manufactured in China on acid-free paper | ISBN 9780525555858 | 10 9 8 7 6

Designed by Jason Henry | Text set in Triplex | The artwork for this book was created digitally.

The publisher does not have any control over and does not assume any responsibility for author or third-party websites or their content.